HOW HOCKEY WORKS

Keltie Thomas

Illustrations by Greg Hall

MAPLE
TREE
PRESS

Maple Tree Press Inc.
51 Front Street East, Suite 200, Toronto, Ontario M5E 1B3
www.mapletreepress.com

Distributed in Canada by Raincoast Books
9050 Shaughnessy Street, Vancouver, British Columbia V6P 6E5

Distributed in the United States by Publishers Group West
1700 Fourth Street, Berkeley, California 94710

Acknowledgments
Special thanks to the Air Canada Centre, Roger Ellis, Paul Gillette, Steve Bodolay, Stephanie Boyd, Blaine Hoshizaki, Craig Johnson, Doug Herridge, Larry Dick, Jim Bowman, Sophie Higgins, Dylan Kristy, the Hockey Hall of Fame, Phil Pritchard, Craig Campbell, Andrew Rutenberg, Jet Ice, everyone at Maple Tree Press, and, of course, P-J.

Cataloguing in Publication Data
Thomas, Keltie
How hockey works / Keltie Thomas ; illustrations by Greg Hall.

Includes index.
ISBN-13: 978-1-897066-64-5 (bound) / ISBN-10: 1-897066-64-3 (bound).
ISBN-13: 978-1-897066-65-2 (pbk.) / ISBN-10: 1-897066-65-1 (pbk.)

1. Hockey—Juvenile literature. I. Hall, Greg, 1963- II. Title.

GV847.25.T48 2006   j796.962   C2004-904658-6

Design & art direction: Greg Hall
Illustrations: Greg Hall
Photo Credits: See page 64

We acknowledge the financial support of the Canada Council for the Arts, the Ontario Arts Council, the Government of Canada through the Book Publishing Industry Development Program (BPIDP), and the Government of Ontario through the Ontario Media Development Corporation's Book Initiative for our publishing activities.

Printed in Belgium

A   B   C   D   E   F

Contents

How Does Hockey Work?

Fans, players, and inquiring minds everywhere want to know!

What makes hockey the coolest and the fastest game on earth? Why is the ice so slippery? What makes a slapshot such a boom with zoom? Why is the puck so shifty? What makes Wayne Gretzky the greatest one of all? How do Zambonis work? What makes a hockey stick feel right? How fast can players rush from end to end? How do goalies play the angle? And what is that angle? What's the score on scoring goals?

Well, just like everything else on earth, it all comes down to science (plus a few things science hasn't managed to explain yet!). And if you think that makes hockey sound boring, you'd better check what planet you're on. But, hey, why don't you turn the page and check out the world of hockey in action for yourself. Whether you want answers to those burning questions, tips on becoming a better player, the scoop on inside information, or just to have a blast with the game, this book's for you.

Psssst. You don't have to be a hockey maniac to read this book. The Rules and Regs and Hockey Talk are decoded on page 61.

The Night the Puck Was Born

Duck! Here comes the puck! Crack! There it goes, right through the window.

That was the scene in the 1800s, one of the first indoor games in Montreal: two teams going at it with a bouncy rubber ball—what was often used then—that kept flying over the boards. Hundreds of dollars in windows had been broken in the first few games at the Victoria Skating Rink. And it was dangerous for fans sitting in the stands.

The owner of the rink was fed up. He snatched the ball, cut off the top and bottom with a jack knife, and threw the middle part back onto the ice. Did he have a hunch that the flat disk would slide across the ice instead of bouncing? Maybe. For as the players went on playing no more windows were shattered. And because the new shape bounced less, it was easier for players to control. So this puck stuck in the game!

Chapter 1

Playing on Thin Ice

**Zing!** The puck skids down the ice at 160 kilometers (100 mi) per hour or more. Swish! Swish! Players rush from end to end of the rink in seconds flat.

What makes hockey the fastest—and the coolest—game on earth?

The ice, of course!

Ice is frozen water and it's slippery stuff. Just think of the last time an ice cube slipped through your fingers. It's not that ice is "too cool to handle." It's that ice is just plain slippery.

The slipperiness of ice helps the puck slide and players glide across the rink. As players' skate blades rub against the ice, the slipperiness cuts down on friction, the force that slows them down. So the slipperiness of ice gives the players and the puck more speed.

And just what makes ice so slippery? Turn the page to check out the slippery science of ice.

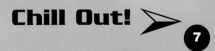

If you're wondering what makes ice so slippery, you're not alone—it's been a mystery for more than 150 years. Until recently, it sparked hot debate among scientists.

Some scientists said skate blades slip on ice because the pressure of the skate blade melts a thin layer on the surface into water. The skates glide across the water, which refreezes almost instantly. Other scientists said the friction created between ice and skates as they rub against each other gives off heat that melts that thin layer into water. It turns out both sides were wrong! Skate blades don't put enough pressure on ice to melt it. And the heat from friction isn't enough to melt ice at the coldest temperatures people can skate in.

So what's up with ice? Recent research shows that a thin "water-like" liquid covers its surface. Although it sounds unbelievable, this liquid is there even at temperatures way below 0°C (32°F), the freezing point of water. And that's what makes ice so slippery.

All Ice Is Not Created Equal

Fast Ice = Good Ice

Hockey players talk about "fast ice." It's hard and smooth, making it easy for players to pass, skate, and play fast. Players like it a lot! The secret to keeping fast ice is to keep it cold.

Slow Ice = Bad Ice

Slow ice is warmer and softer than fast ice. More "snow," or ice shavings from players' skates piles up on it, making the surface rougher and slowing down the game.

Hockey Ice ≠ Figure-skating Ice

Hockey players skate on ice that's only 2.5 cm (1 in) thick. Figure skaters like ice that's about 5 cm (2 in) thick. They also prefer softer ice than hockey ice, so that it "gives" more when they land their jumps, which gives the figure skaters more control.

Playoffs

During the 1999 Stanley Cup playoff final between the Dallas Stars and the Buffalo Sabres, the ice in Dallas got so soft and mushy that some players said it felt like skating on a Slurpee™!

Stanley Cup

Quick Shot

Hockey players played on the "world's fastest ice" at the 2002 Olympics, and speed skaters broke several records on it! What made the ice so fast? State-of-the-art equipment, reduced air resistance at the rink's high altitude, and purified water, which cuts down friction between ice and skate blades.

Hockey's Ice Ages

1859 The Big Chill

Take a look at your fridge. It's one of the most important inventions in hockey. Imagine it wasn't around—if you brought a chunk of ice inside in the middle of winter, it would melt into a puddle of water, right? When refrigeration was perfected in 1859, it became possible to keep ice frozen indoors. Before long, indoor rinks were built and hockey could be played inside. The game no longer depended on the weather, and players weren't slowed down by high-speed winds blowing against them.

1940 The Fast Floods

It didn't seem like a big deal when the NHL made a rule that the ice had to be well cleaned and flooded, or resurfaced, between game periods. But it had a huge impact. Players no longer found their skates sinking into ice that got softer and softer as the game went on. And the game didn't have to be stopped constantly to fix cracks in the ice that got chippier and chippier. So the pace of the game got faster and faster!

1947 The Whiteout

White paint made the puck a TV star. It was the year before hockey hit the tube, and judging goals was a tough job. Instant replays weren't around to help referees and goal judges tell whether goals had been scored. The NHL made a rule that the ice in and around the net had to be painted white to make the puck easier to see. The paint was a splashy success with refs and fans. So the next year, when hockey was first shown on TV, all the ice was painted white to make the puck more visible on the tube. And this made the puck much easier to see on the rink, too.

Ice Rink White

Though the ice hockey players skate on is only 2.5 cm (1 in) thick, depending on who you talk to, it can take anywhere from 24 hours to two days to make from scratch. Here's how the ice-making crew at the Air Canada Centre does it.

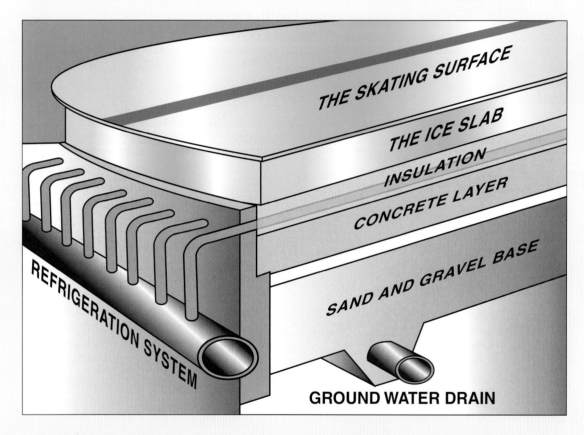

THE SKATING SURFACE

THE ICE SLAB

INSULATION

CONCRETE LAYER

SAND AND GRAVEL BASE

REFRIGERATION SYSTEM

GROUND WATER DRAIN

1. The crew cools the rink to about 16°C (61°F).

2. The refrigeration system chills the ice slab—the concrete floor the ice is built on—by pumping freezing salty water through pipes in the slab. This cools the slab to about 0°C (32°F) so that water will freeze on it.

3. The crew sprays pure water onto the slab to make a layer of ice that will stick to the slab.

4. Layer by layer, the crew builds up the ice with water until it's about 0.3 cm (1/8 in) thick. Then they paint it white. (Up until this point, you can see the gray concrete floor right through the ice!)

5. The crew continues to build up the ice until it's about 0.6 cm (1/4 in) thick. Then they paint on the center-ice line, blue lines, faceoff circles, and goal creases.

6. Still building up the ice, the crew paints on the team and company logos. After that, they seal the paint, using a process called "pebbling." Pebbling creates a surface on the paint that the ice on top can grip.

7. When the ice is 1.8 to 2.5 cm (3/4–1 in) thick, it's ready for a game. The Air Canada Centre crew likes to go with ice that's about 1.8 cm (3/4 in) thick rather than 2.5 cm (1 in). Why? Because the thinner the ice is, the easier it is to control its temperature.

Beware the Beast

Maybe the ice plant at Toronto's Air Canada Centre should have a sign on it that says "Enter at your own risk." After all, the "Beast," as the refrigeration system is affectionately dubbed by the Centre's ice-making staff, lurks within. It's a big blue hulk of metal that looks like a space alien with three heads, three bodies, and arms that shoot off in all directions. And when it's in chill mode, it even squeals like an alien. It's made of three high-tech compressors that can pump out 675 tons of refrigeration to make and chill ice 24 hours a day, 7 days a week. Maybe it should be called a serial chiller!

Keeping the ice cool once it's made is like trying to keep a giant ice cube in a freezer that's full of holes and hot air. The doors of the rink are constantly opening as people come and go. And during games, hot TV lights beam down on the ice, while the body heat of 18,000 fans or more surrounds it. So a crew of engineers work with high-tech tools: two sensors in the ice slab measure the ice's temperature at the concrete floor; an infrared camera 40 m (132 feet) above the ice records the surface temperature and condition of the ice. The readings are fed into a computer that controls the Beast. The engineers check the readings on the computer, and then they adjust the amount of refrigeration that the Beast huffs and puffs out to cool down or warm up the ice as needed.

Quick Shot

It takes about 45,455 L (10,000 ga) of water to make 2.5 cm (1 in) of ice for a standard hockey rink. That's about 455 bathtubs full!

Star ⭐

Cammi Granato, the all-time leading scorer of the U.S. women's team, said the best part of her game is the way she sees the ice. If you keep your eye on the puck, looking for a chance to score, you can be like Granato and always show up right where the action is.

Cammi Granato

Quick Shot

When a Canadian ice maker made the ice for the 2002 Olympics, he secretly stashed a loonie at center ice. And that Canadian dollar coin just may have brought the Canadian women and men's hockey teams luck, for when they skated on it they both won gold!

The Zamboni

A Zamboni is like a huge razor blade on wheels with a built-in towel on the end. It gives the ice a close shave to resurface it. This helps stop chipping, which can make the puck bounce and skates wobble, and it makes the ice fresh and smooth for players. Here's how the big hunk of 'boni does it.

1 The Shave

The big blade shaves the surface of the ice. How much ice does it cut off? It all depends on the state of the ice. The rougher it is, the more the blade shaves off.

2 Whisking Up the Shavings

A large screw collects the ice shavings, or snow, so they don't pile up on the ice. It feeds them into the snow tank at the front of the Zamboni and later they're dumped out.

3 Washing Up

The Zamboni cruises around with two water tanks. As the blade shaves, water from the wash-water tank flows to a squeegee-like conditioner behind the blade, which smooths the ice and floods it with the wash water to flush dirt out of any deep cuts in the ice. The dirty wash water is vacuumed up and any leftover water is squeegeed off.

4 The Hot Towel Finish

A huge towel behind the conditioner spreads hot, clean water from the second water tank. The hot water softens any ruts or grooves in the ice and fills them in to make the ice surface smooth when the water freezes.

Where does the word "Zamboni" come from?

The Zamboni gets its name from its inventor. Frank Zamboni invented it in the 1940s out of an old jeep and tires designed to grip ice.

What did they do before the Zamboni rolled onto the scene?

A team of up to ten people shoveled snow off the ice, and another team pulled barrels of water to coat it with hot water. The Zamboni turned the job of resurfacing into a one-person operation.

How fast does a Zamboni go?

Even at its top speed, a Zamboni moves only as fast as a slow tractor. Experts say the ultimate ice job takes about seven to seven-and-a-half laps around a standard size rink.

Are Zambonis hard to drive?

While you drive, you can barely see over the front, and there are 12 things to adjust. And you have to get the job done between periods!

The Daily Grind

First Zamboni, © 1945.

Scrape! Scratch! Gouge! The ice takes a real beating every game from players' skates and sticks, and bits of debris. Zambonis resurface the ice between periods and games to fill up its ruts and cuts. They shave it to cut it down and flood it to build it back up. Some areas need a closer shave than others, and some need a thicker flood than others. That means the thickness of the ice is constantly in flux. So every day, engineers check the overall thickness with a drill. They drill down at 20 different spots to bring up cores of ice they can measure. This gives them the big picture of the whole cube. If the ice is too thin in spots, they tell the Zamboni drivers to flood these areas with more water. And if it's too thick in spots, they tell the drivers to shave down these areas.

Quick Shot

Ever noticed that the Zamboni misses spots on the ice? Some Zamboni drivers call these gaps "vacations" or "holidays," depending on how big the gap is.

Home Ice

If the ice in the Air Canada Centre in Toronto, Ontario, were cut up into 2.5 cm (1 in) cubes, you'd end up with 2 million ice cubes!

13

Scott Mellanby

It's Raining Rats and Rats

The year was 1995 and the Florida Panthers were getting ready for the home-opener of their third NHL season. Suddenly, a rat bolted across the dressing-room floor. Forward Scott Mellanby grabbed his stick and slapped the rat as if it were a puck. Then Scott went out and scored two goals in a 4–3 win over the Calgary Flames.

"He came in the next day," John Vanbiesbrouck, the Panthers' goalie, said "and I gave him the line, 'It wasn't a hat trick, but it was a rat trick.'" The next time Scott scored, a fan threw a plastic rat on the ice. And after that, it became "the year of the rat." Every time the Panthers scored, fans tossed thousands of plastic rats onto the ice. Arena staff scurried to clear them. Games were delayed. Fears were raised for players' safety. But the team played on and the rats seemed to help. For the first time, the Panthers made it all the way to the final playoff round.

Not impressed by the rat rain, the League made the rule that no object can be thrown on the ice. But fans got around it by pitching the plastic rodents on the ice *after* the game. So rats still rule!

Great Skate, *Fast Player*

Swish!

What do you do more than anything else when you play hockey? Skate! Passing, shooting, checking, or covering your opponent, you're skating on two thin steel blades. Skating is the most basic skill of hockey. You build all your other skills on top of it.

If you can't skate well, you won't go very far! Experts say poor skating is the main thing that keeps players out of pro hockey. And good skaters are hard to find because few players ever develop the correct technique.

Skaters like Scott Niedermayer and Alexander Ovechkin make it look easy. They stride down the ice with posture good for balance and speed: head up, knees and ankles bent, waist leaning slightly forward, and weight on the balls of the feet. They zigzag, start, stop, pivot, and turn and go flat out at breakneck speed—as fast as six to ten meters (20–30 ft) per second. That speed could be a winning edge. Check out the science of great skating and skates!

Turn on a dime ➤

Speedy Skating

Name one hockey player who doesn't want to be a Speedster on skates! Speed can get you to the puck ahead of your opponents and leave them in the dust, so you can carry the puck into their end for a shot on goal. Speed comes from power. To skate faster, check out the science behind the "power points" of your stride.

There are three kinds of skating in hockey:

Free skating (or straight-away skating) is the speedy skating hockey players use on open ice.

Agility skating —quick stops and starts, bursts of speed, fast changes of direction, and changes of pace to dodge oncoming checkers—is a must for a stop-and-go game like hockey.

Backward skating is not just for defense players in a game that switches fast from offense to defense. If an opponent intercepts your pass and rushes toward you, you can switch into reverse to cover the opponent without taking your eyes off the puck.

What's key to all three types of hockey skating? Balance, balance, balance! Proper balance spreads your weight evenly over your skates, giving you greater speed, greater maneuverability, and the ability to take body checks without falling down. It's mainly controlled by the position of your upper body above your skates. But it can take months—even years—of practice to learn balance. After all, you are skating on blades that are only millimeters thick and, with each stride you take, you're shifting your weight from one foot to the other. But don't let that throw you off balance! The more you practice skating, the better your balance will become.

Power Up the Push Off

As you push off at the beginning of a stride, you dig your blade into the ice. Since the friction between blade and ice gives you speed, the harder you press into the ice, the faster you will go. Lean forward (so you don't lose pushing force by moving up instead of forward) and put your whole body weight into your pushing leg. Tilt your foot so the inside edge of your blade makes a 45° angle with the ice to dig in harder.

Extend Your Speed

As you push off, your foot comes off the ice. But lifting it too high wastes energy, throws off your balance, and cuts down your speed. Lift your foot just above the ice (shown here). Now follow through by extending your leg behind you and locking your knee. If you don't extend your leg fully before you take another stride, you lose power from your push off and can't reach your top speed.

Return to Your Speed Center

To get the most power from the next push off, both feet must be centered under your body. Think of this spot as your speed center. To get there, bring your leg back quickly and keep your foot as close to the ice as possible. Otherwise, you may bounce up and lose speed as your other leg takes a stride. Now you're ready to push off on your other leg. Go for it!

Goalie Grrl Crashes Guy's Game

Play hockey in figure skates and you're likely to catch a toepick in the ice—then faceplant. Ouch! Just ask Manon Rheaume (pictured at right in goal).

Canada's 1998 Olympic team goalie played her first hockey game in figure skates when she was five. Back then, her brother's team needed a goalie and Manon talked her parents into letting her do the job. Her figure skates made her wobble, the goalie leg pads tripped her up, and the gloves were big enough to swim in. But she was hooked. After the game, Rheaume asked her father to file the picks off the tips of her skate blades so she wouldn't trip.

Right then and there, she decided she wanted to play goal in the big leagues. She kept playing with the boys and, when she was 20, she got the chance. In 1992, Phil Esposito, General Manager of the Tampa Bay Lightning, invited her to training camp. During the camp, she played between the pipes for the Lightning in a pre-season game. And that's how Rheaume crashed the guys' game and became the first woman to play in the NHL. Today, Rheaume helps develop hockey skates and equipment just for women. Go grrl!

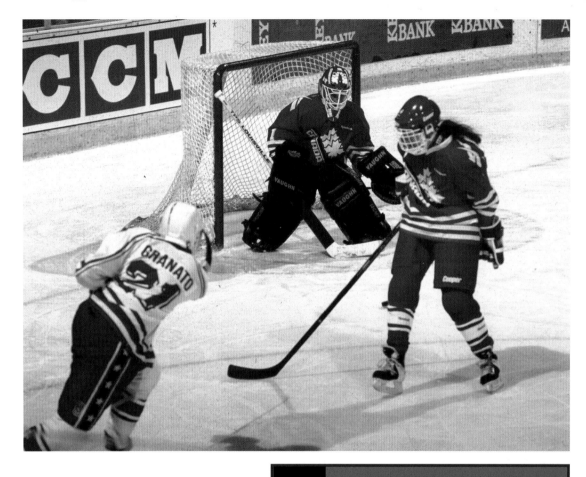

Quick Shot

What's power skating? Just call it skating for speed. It's when you apply maximum power and science against the ice to build the highest speed in the shortest length of time.

Tip

Twenty-five percent of skating speed is brain power. If you think about pushing yourself past the natural habit of taking it easy, you'll skate faster. Try it!

Great Skates

Skates have come a long way since they were invented. The oldest skates ever found are 3,000 years old and they're made of animal bone! Ancient people of Scandinavia sharpened wood and bones from elk, reindeer, and caribou and strapped them onto their boots to go hunting. Since bone and wood don't glide well on ice, the ancient hunters used poles like ski poles to push themselves along as they skated. Today, pro hockey skates are made of high-tech materials to deliver control and speed on ice.

Bullet-Proof Skin

The skin of pro skate boots is made of the same stuff as bullet-proof vests—tightly woven, extra-strength nylon. It provides support and protects players' feet from cuts. Hey, lots of sharp blades are out there on the ice!

Wobble-Proof Ankles

Everybody knows that wobbly ankles are a no-no. Some pro skates have ankles made of as many as six layers for support. A stiff ankle piece holds the foot in place and a gel-filled sac molds around the ankle to give players better control as they skate.

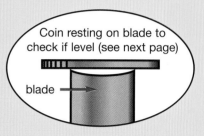

Coin resting on blade to check if level (see next page)

blade

Blades of Steel

Skate blades are made of stainless steel to keep a sharp edge under rough and tough use. The bottom of each blade has a groove, or hollow, with a knifelike edge on each side—an inside edge and an outside edge. The edges cut into the ice to give you a good grip on the ice. They allow you to dig into the ice for power, speed, and control. In fact, the ice should feel anything but slippery under these blades of steel!

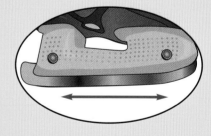

Ultra Light for Flight

Carrying extra weight around slows players down. So pro skates are made of the lightest materials possible. Since feet sweat and ice shavings melt, many of these materials wick away moisture to keep skates light and waterlog-free.

Hold 'er Steady

The blade holder holds the blade on the boot. As you skate, it transfers the energy from your foot to the blade, so it's made of materials like Kevlar, graphite, and plastic that don't bend. Otherwise, some of your energy will be lost. Not to mention speed and maybe even your balance!

Fits Like a Glove

Skates usually fit one to one-and-a-half sizes smaller than street shoes. If they're too big, energy from your foot will be lost as your foot moves around in the boot. So inflatable sacs and foam pads mold skates to the shape of your feet. This maximizes the energy that goes from your feet to the blades.

The Rocker

A rocker, or curve, on the bottom of your blades helps you make turns. The bigger the rocker, the more the maneuverability you have, but the less power and speed, because only part of the blade makes contact with the ice. So players choose how much to "rock" based on their personal playing style.

How are skates sharpened?

The blades are passed over a wheel that spins with a diamond tip on it. The hard tip makes a groove in the blade, so the edges can grip the ice.

How can you tell if your skates are sharpened well?

Lay a quarter along the bottom of the blade. Take a good look at the angle of the coin. If it's completely level, the edges are even and ready for action. But if it leans to one side, one edge is higher than the other, and this will interfere with your skating. Then you need to get your blade resharpened.

How much "bite" is right?

The deeper the hollow, the more bite, or grip, you have on the ice, but the less speed and glide. Goalies like hardly any bite at all so they can move easily from side to side.

Quick Shot

Players skate about three to five kilometers (2–3 mi) a game. And if the coach makes poor line changes, they may log in an extra couple of kilometers on top of that!

Skating through Time

1000 BC

Skate blades are made out of animal bones.

1300s

Wooden skates that have long, wide runners instead of blades appear.

1850

The most popular skates in North America have a wooden base and a metal blade that curls up at the front. The first hockey skates are made around this time.

1860

Hockey skate blades are made with a rocker to give players better maneuverabiltiy. Though most hockey players wear clamp-on skates, more and more start to realize that skates that screw onto their boots give them more stability and are less likely to come loose during a game.

1900

Around this time, special hockey boots are made of leather.

1905

Skates with reinforced toe and heel caps are made for goalies. Eventually, the protective caps are added to all hockey skates.

1960s

Hockey skates are made with protective foam pad linings and ankle guards. Around this time, the first plastic skate boots are made.

2002

Rip! Rip! German and Czech Olympic players compete in skates that sound like paper tearing as they slice across the ice. The blades are thinner than regular ones so they heat up faster, which is said to cut down gliding friction by an incredible 40 percent!

Pavel Bure

How Dull Blades Turned into a Sharp Edge

Va-voom! There goes the Russian Rocket. Rightwinger Pavel Bure is one lean, mean skating machine. Experts say he has excellent skating technique—correct posture, balance, and speed. But it wasn't always so.

Bure once told a hockey reporter that when he started playing hockey as a kid he wasn't a very good skater. At his first hockey practice, he could barely skate at all. Every time he tried to move, he fell down. He was embarrassed and so was his father, who was a well-known Olympic swimmer. Pavel's father said that if he didn't practice and become the best skater there in a few months, they weren't going back.

Turns out Bure's dad didn't realize that skates need to be sharpened. Pavel's blades were so dull that they couldn't grip the ice. No wonder he kept falling down! But the experience made a sharp impression on Bure. He practiced skating almost every chance he got and today he's one of the best skaters in the NHL.

Chapter 3

That's the Way the Puck Bounces

Bounce!

Everybody knows that hockey is a sport that's "not on the ball." Instead, it's played with a small rubber puck that slides, bounces, rolls, and rebounds as players chase it around the ice. Everybody wants to get a piece of it, and fans can't take their eyes off it. The whole game is stuck on the puck!

According to the rules of the game, the puck must be kept in motion at all times. In players' quest to put it in the net, they whack it, shoot it, pass it, stickhandle it, and shove it. The puck absorbs the energy put into these puck-handling moves to slide across the ice or fly through the air. How does the puck take such a beating and keep on trucking, er, "pucking?" And can a game be won or lost on the way the puck bounces? It all comes down to what the puck is made of.

Bounce on in! ➤

What makes this slippery character so hard to pin down?

It's bouncy.

No matter how you whack at it, bang it along the boards, or fire it into a goalpost, the puck always bounces back. That's because it's made out of rubber—one of the most springy materials in the world. The molecules, or building blocks, of rubber have a structure that gives it this extraordinary bounciness, or resilience.

It's cool.

Forget cool, dude. The puck is frozen solid. Pucks are put in the freezer before NHL games and even between periods. Why? To numb some of its bounciness, so players can maneuver it more easily. Freezing the puck takes heat, or stored energy, out of it. Then it can't bounce as much or as high. This makes it slide across the ice better and easier for players to stickhandle, pass, and shoot.

It's got dimples.

Ever noticed the tiny dimples or grooves on the sides of the puck? They're set in a pattern that looks like a tire tread. The dimples roughen up the sides of the puck. Then, when a player's stick rubs against the sides, friction is created. And friction lightly holds the puck to the player's stick.

It's hard-headed.

Rubber bands are soft and squishy. So if the puck is made out of rubber, how come it's anything but? The puck is made out of hardened, or vulcanized, rubber just like car tires. This makes it stronger and more elastic so that it can go head to head with the boards, sticks, and skates over and over without cracking up or getting bent out of shape.

It stays in shape.

NHL pucks are checked for size, weight, and rebound, so they have to hold their shape. Only top-quality rubber goes into big-league pucks. If you stretch a piece of rubber, it will snap back to its original length. But pucks with cheap filler material lose some of this "snap back" quality. Then they won't pass the rebound test.

It's flashy.

Ever notice how the puck seems to disappear on TV? Over the years, the puck's been colored to make it more visible, but paints wore off, and dyes faded or made the puck mushy. In 1996, the Fox TV network launched a puck with built-in electronic tracking. Whenever it reached high speeds, it signaled a device to leave a red trail on the screen. But it was just a flash in the pan!

Making a Batch of Rubber Pies

Believe it or not, making a thousand pucks is a bit like making a batch of black rubber pies. You start by mixing the ingredients—rubber, carbon black or coal dust, and sulfur. Carbon black makes the rubber stronger and stiffer, and also gives the puck its black color. Sulfur vulcanizes, or hardens, rubber when it's baked and makes it more elastic.

A big, automatic mixer blends the ingredients together. Then motorized rollers roll out the rubbery mixture into flat sheets. A machine shapes the sheets into long, soft rubber logs, which are sliced into disks like pies. The pies are put into molding presses that look a bit like muffin tins. Then they're baked for 20 minutes. When the pucks pop out of the molds, they've got dimples on the sides. Then they're ready to have team logos put on them and get in the game.

When people other than goalies get their hands on the puck during a game, things can get too hot handle— especially the puck. Here's the science behind the rules of "puckhandling."

Gotta Hand It to You, Fred!

Under pressure in your own end? Can't shoot the puck out? In the 1920s, Fred "Cyclone" Taylor of the Vancouver Millionaires had the perfect solution to this problem. He just picked up the puck and lobbed it into the crowd, throwing the puck right out of the game! Fred's unique "puckhandling" maneuver was so effective at stopping the game that other players began using it, too. But in 1928 the NHL made the rule that no player but the goalie can close his hand on the puck.

A Hot Scam

Back in the old days of the NHL, the home team's trainer was in charge of keeping spare pucks frozen in a bucket of snow and ready to go. But during the 1964–65 season, the League noticed something funny going on. If the play heated up in the last few minutes of a tight game, so did the puck. If the home team was fighting to hang on to a one-goal lead, say, it would flip the puck into the stands. The trainer would quite often get a replacement puck from the coach's pocket, where it had been warming up on the sly. So the League decided to put the score keepers in charge of all the pucks used in the game.

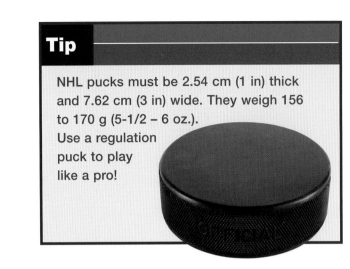

Chilling on Ice

Whenever there's a faceoff in a game, an official holds the puck and drops it onto the ice. But if he holds the puck for too long, it can absorb heat from his hand and warm right up. Then it will bounce wildly when it's back in play. So whenever a team calls a timeout or it's time for a TV commercial break, officials put the puck down on the ice to keep its cool!

Quick Shot

No puck? No problem. Over the years, hockey players have whacked away at tin cans, India rubber balls, lacrosse balls, frozen apples, coal, wood, and even frozen chunks of horse manure!

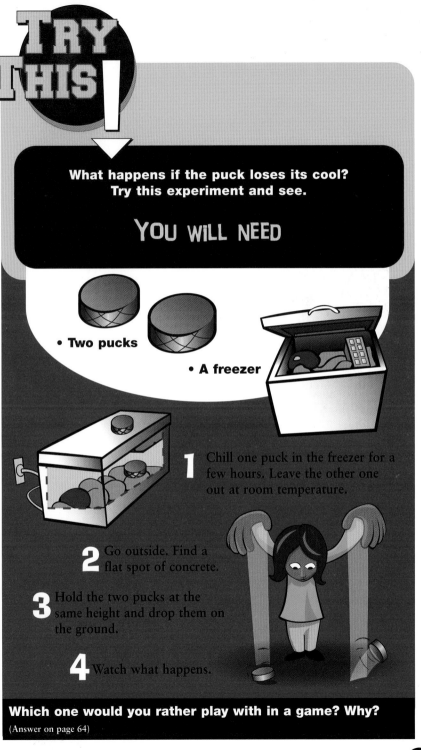

TRY THIS!

What happens if the puck loses its cool? Try this experiment and see.

YOU WILL NEED

- **Two pucks**
- **A freezer**

1 Chill one puck in the freezer for a few hours. Leave the other one out at room temperature.

2 Go outside. Find a flat spot of concrete.

3 Hold the two pucks at the same height and drop them on the ground.

4 Watch what happens.

Which one would you rather play with in a game? Why?

(Answer on page 64)

Fred Waghorne

When the Puck Came Unglued

One night in 1900 the puck went to pieces. In those days the puck wasn't made as solidly as it is today. It was made out of two pieces of rubber stuck together with glue.

A couple of teams were squaring off in Belleville, Ontario. A player let a shot go on net. The puck struck the goalpost, and it split right in two. One half bounced off into the boards, and the other half sailed straight into the net!

Was it a goal? Well, just like the puck, the opinion of the two teams was split right down the middle. But referee Fred Waghorne was of one mind about it. He whipped out his rulebook and pointed to the rule that says the puck must be 2.54 cm (1 in) thick. Since the puck in the net wasn't this thick, he ruled it wasn't a legal puck. So no goal was scored. After that, it was decided that the puck should be made of one piece of rubber and it's been made like that to this day.

Chapter 4

Tricky Sticky Science

Very Picky!

That's how players are about their sticks. In a set of 24 sticks, only six may meet the performance demands of a pro. The fact is, hockey sticks have to perform under extreme conditions without cracking up. They're constantly scraping against the ice, bumping into the boards, and slapping the puck. Not to mention getting hit by the puck every time you receive a pass or stop the black 'n' bruising disk with it.

When players pick up a stick, they know whether it "feels right." The Great One, Wayne Gretzky, liked his sticks to be stiff and light with a medium curve in the blade. Generally, players look for lightness, stiffness, and balance in a stick. But what's right for one player can be completely different for another. Players' sticks are as individual as their signatures. They vary in weight, length, blade shape and curve, and what they're made of—aluminum, wood, or graphite. In fact, stick makers store individual players' stick patterns on computers to make custom sticks for the pros. Get a feel for the picky science of sticks.

Stickhandle this way ➤

Pick a Stick

If you think a hockey stick is like an everyday broomstick, think again. It's a finely tuned instrument that can make the puck zoom across the ice two or three times faster than the speediest skater. You maneuver it to pass the puck to your teammates, to carry the puck as you dodge oncoming checkers, and to fire shots on net. The best sticks work as if they're an extension of your arms that have the touch-sensitivity of your fingertips. Here's the science behind what makes a stick "feel right."

The Whippy Factor

Don't get shafted when you choose a new a stick. Make sure it's whippy. According to the pros, a shaft's whippiness, or flexibility, is the most important thing to consider in choosing a stick, since it determines how much energy the stick absorbs and transfers to the puck when you shoot. If a shaft is too stiff for you, it won't bend as much and less of your energy will go into the stick. This will cut down on the speed and accuracy of your shots and give you "less feel for the puck." Likewise, if the shaft's too springy, it'll bend too much, reducing your puck control and your feel for the puck, as well as the accuracy of your shots. So how do you tell if the flexibility of a shaft is right for you? Try bending it in the store. If you can bend it with medium effort, the whippiness is just right.

The Long and Short of It

The length of your stick mainly depends on your height. Experts say it's the right length if it touches the tip of your nose when you're in standing in sock feet. But you need to make sure it feels right when you're on the ice. Some players choose lengths that help them do their job. For example, some forwards find short sticks help them stickhandle better, because short sticks allow them to carry the puck closer to their body. On the other hand, some defense players like long sticks that give them a longer reach to jab the puck away from goal-hungry opponents. In the 1920s, defenseman Ernie "Moose" Johnson played with the longest stick in hockey— 190 cm (75 in) long! But the NHL outlawed it, and today no stick can be more than 160 cm (63 in) long.

Layer It On

Layers of graphite Kevlar, fiberglass, and other strong, light materials strengthen the shaft of many wood sticks.

Tip

To see if you're using the right lie, look at the bottom of the blade on a stick you've used a lot. If the bottom is worn evenly, it's the right lie. If it's more worn on the heel, you need a bigger angle. If it's more worn on the toe, you need a smaller angle. The right lie allows the blade to lay flat on the ice when you're playing and stickhandling.

Curved to Perfection

Some players use blowtorches, rasps, or hacksaws to shape their stickblades into the "perfect" curve! A curved blade helps players lift the puck off the ice and can make their shots dip and sway through the air so goalies can't tell where they'll end up. But too big a curve makes it tough to get away a backhand shot.

Built-in Sweet Spot

Some blades have a built-in sweet spot, or area that makes the most effective contact with the puck, made of strong materials, such as Kevlar and graphite.

How to Tell a Lie

The angle between the heel of the blade and the shaft is called the lie. Its size can affect the power and accuracy of your shot. For example, a big angle can give you more power, because it gives you a longer sweep and follow through when you shoot. On the other hand, a small angle can give your shots more accuracy, because the puck is closer to your feet, which gives you more control. But the angle that's right for you depends on your skating and puck-carrying style. A big angle suits players who skate close to the ice and carry the puck out in front of them, while a small angle suits players who skate upright and carry the puck near their feet.

Does Your Blade Make the Grade?

The blade has to stay stiff and strong, without cracking, under pressure. It's the part of the stick that makes the most contact with the ice and the puck. Stick makers use materials like fiberglass and carbon to reinforce the strength of the blade without adding weight to the stick.

Tape It Up

Taping your blade gives you a better grip on the puck. The rough surface of tape increases the friction between the blade and the puck's dimples, which lightly holds the puck to the stick. Tape also keeps the blade dry. This is important if you have a wooden blade, because wood warps and becomes soft when it gets wet. But don't go ape on the tape—one layer will do. More than one will make your stick heavier to carry, which can slow you down. Start taping at the heel of the blade and tape your way to the end.

Wax Job

To get better puck control, some players put stick wax on their tape. The wax stops snow from the ice from sticking to the tape and making it wet.

Sticky Business

L ong gone are the days when players lopped off a tree branch and carved themselves a stick out of it. Today, more than 20 different steps go into making a wooden hockey stick—from drying the wood to cutting and sanding it. And more than 50 steps go into a goalie stick! Not only that, stick makers use computers and robots in the process, constantly experimenting with new materials and production methods in search of the perfect stick.

Time's Stick Picks

1850s

Alexander Rutherford of Lindsay, Ontario, carves a hockey stick out of a hickory tree branch. When Gord Sharpe, Alexander's great, great grandson, has it valued for insurance purposes 150 years later, he discovers it's the oldest hockey stick in the world—worth a cool $2 million.

1900s

William Holborn, owner of the American Plough Works in Ayr, Ontario, must have been mad about hockey. For somehow, he discovered his machine for making wooden plow handles could make hock-ey sticks. The plow handle business went bust in 1920, but Hilborn was making hockey sticks out of hard rock elm wood for department stores and sporting good companies. In 1928, he made the world's first two-piece hockey stick.

1960s

"Wood-n't" it be nice to make a hockey stick that didn't crack under pressure? Hockey stick blades were often made of rock elm and the shafts of ash, which was stiff enough to bend and then snap back into position as players shot. In the late '60s, stick companies began strengthening blades and shafts with fiberglass to help the sticks last longer and resist cracking under slapshots.

1970s

When the first sticks made of laminate wood, or thin strips of wood glued together, appeared on the scene, they weren't always up to snuff. When a trainload of the sticks, bound to outfit the entire Western Canada Junior League, froze on the way, the glue went brittle. And the whole shipment was wrecked. Once players got their hands on them the sticks broke like wooden matches! But stick makers stuck with the glue, experimenting with it until they got it right.

1980s

When Wayne Gretzky gave up his wood stick for a new-fangled aluminum one, loads of pros checked them out and followed his lead. Aluminum is stiffer and lighter than wood, so it lets players put more of their energy into their shot and release the puck more quickly. And it doesn't get soft, so it provides a more consistent shot. But aluminum sticks are too stiff for kids under 11, and many players find that wood sticks give them a better "feel" for the puck.

2001

More than 100 NHLers trade in their sticks for a new one-piece stick made of graphite and Kevlar. At 460 grams (1 lb), the stick weighs half as much as a wooden one. And players can load more energy into its shaft than almost any other kind of stick—that energy gets put into the puck. Some players say the stick gives them a quicker release and harder shot. But others say nothing will ever replace the "feel" of wood.

Quick Answers to Speedy Questions

What superstitions do NHL stars have about their sticks?

The Great One, Wayne Gretzky, didn't like his hockey sticks to touch any other sticks or to cross one another. "I kind of have them hidden in the corner," he once said.

Darcy Tucker uses an aluminum stick with a wooden blade. When he sits on the bench, Tucker always has the blade facing up so he can "knock on wood" if a bad thought crosses his mind.

Jeremy Roenick never lets anyone touch his sticks. If someone touches one of his sticks even by accident, he'll throw it out or give it away. Before each game, Roenick assembles his sticks—putting the blades and shafts together—and tapes them just how he likes them. Hey, when you have a routine that works, you have to "stick" with it!

If Gordie Howe, one of hockey's goal-scoring greats, thought a teammate's stick had "some lucky goals in it," he'd borrow it in a flash.

Grab for Graphite

You won't find Stephanie Boyd shooting with a wooden stick. According to the former Team USA center who plays in the Women's National Hockey League and runs a hockey school for girls, graphite sticks are the only kind she'll handle. Lots of players use graphite sticks because they perform the same way every time. "If you have two graphite sticks," Stephanie says, "they will be very similar, and when you shoot the puck, the sticks will react the same." She likes graphite sticks because they can be made "so that the puck will always come off the stick at the same point at the same speed." That's a stick to rely on!

Quick Shot

Since goalies always watch the puck, some players put black tape on their stick blades to try to hide the puck. Sneaky!

Stan Mikita

When Sticks Made the Puck Go Bananas

One day in the 1960s, Stan Mikita, star center of the Chicago Black Hawks, broke his stickblade. Cra-a-ack! The blade twisted and bent. But it was just a practice, so he kept playing with it. And that's when the puck went crazy! Every time Mikita made a pass or shot on net, the puck practically jumped off his stick. It sailed, swooped, and curved through the air. Bobby Hull, nicknamed "The Golden Jet" for his supersonic speed, high-scoring flair, and blond hair, tried Mikita's bent blade and decided he wanted one too.

Mikita and the Golden Jet soaked a blade in water, bent it under a door overnight, and the "banana blade" was born. Its big curve allowed players to give the puck more speed, height, and spin. The banana blade was a goalie's worst nightmare: how can you stop the puck if you can't tell where it's going?

Over the next seven years, Mikita and Hull wielded it to win six scoring championships between them. But eventually, the banana blade lost its "ap-peel." The League thought the blade gave offense an unfair edge over defense. So, they outlawed it. Today, blades can have a curve of no more than half an inch, and the crazy banana blade is no more.

**Rough** **and tough.** Everybody knows that's what hockey is. The ice is hard as rock. The boards are punishing to human flesh and bone. The steel skate blades are razor-sharp. The sticks send the puck whizzing through the air with the force of 560 kg (1250 lb). And hockey is a game of physical contact.

That's why players deck themselves out in protective gear from head to toe. But it wasn't always so. Around 1800, the first players stepped out on the ice with only skates and a stick. In 1890, women played hockey in long skirts and figure skates! As the game developed, so did the gear. And as the gear developed, it changed how the game was played.

**Gear Up!**

Player Gear

Putting on hockey gear is like putting on a suit of armor. You end up covering yourself from head to toe. Do you really need all that protective gear? You bet. It's designed to protect those parts of your body that don't have much padding—your head, elbows, knees, and shins.

1 Jersey

The first sweaters were made of thick wool. They fit tightly to keep players warm as they played outside. Today, jerseys fit loosely. They're made of synthetic mesh fabric that's lightweight and breathable. The fabric is designed to keep players cool and dry under hot TV lights. It keeps out the cold and wicks moisture away from the body.

2 Shin Pads

Shin pads of thick catalogs and books were the first pieces of protective gear players invented to shield themselves from the hard-hitting puck. Until the 1960s, leather and felt shin pads were heavy and offered little protection. Modern-day shin pads protect both the shin bone and the knee with strong crack-resistant plastic that can withstand 160 km/h (100 mph) slapshot blasts. Some have a mesh lining that wicks sweat away from the body and kills bacteria to keep the pads odor-free!

3 Helmet

Never play without a "brain bucket." Today, all pros and amateurs must wear a safety-approved helmet. The hard outer shell of helmets is crash-tested and designed to cut down the force of high-impact hits and falls by spreading out the force over a large area. Inside helmets, squishy foam cushions the head, absorbing the shock of the impact.

4 Neck Guard

Neck guards are made out of bullet-proof nylon for protection from cuts by skates and sticks.

5 Gloves

A good pair of hockey gloves must protect your hands from slashes and cuts without interfering with the grip and feel of your stick. Today, most gloves are made of hard plastic and dense foam padding covered in nylon. Some have "thumb locks," to prevent the thumb from being bent back, and lightweight air sacs that act as shock absorbers to protect the fragile bones in the back of the hand.

6 Groin Protection

Underneath their hockey pants, guys wear a protective cup, also called a jock, made of hard crack-resistant plastic to protect the groin. Gals wear a similar pelvic protector called a jill.

⑦ Face Protection

Players wear a cage like the one at the left or a visor made of clear, crack-resistant plastic. Visors give crucial protection for the eyes. "If I were starting out all over again, I would be wearing a visor," said Wayne Gretzky shortly after Brian Berard, a talented young defense player, was accidentally pierced in the eye with a stick.

⑧ Pants

In the early days, hockey pants were cotton knickers that came below the knee. Later, the pants were made out of canvas, and padding was added. Today, hockey pants are made of light waterproof nylon and dense foam padding. Some include special guards to protect the kidneys, waist, and hips. And some are made with Kevlar around the leg openings, so players can step into them with their skates on without cutting the pants.

⑨ Socks

Players wear long socks held up by a garter belt or velcro on hockey shorts that are worn under their hockey pants.

⑩ Skates

Hockey skates are made out of bullet-proof nylon and are designed to protect players' feet (see Great Skates, p. 18). Players are not allowed to wear speed skates or any other skates with a design that might cause injuries.

⑪ Mouth Guard

A mouth guard gives players protection from injuries to the teeth and jaw, as well as concussions (see Conked in the Head, p. 43). It's made out of heat-sensitive dental vinyl. Before using it, you boil it in water for several seconds and then bite down on it to mold it around your teeth.

⑫ Shoulder Pads

Not only do shoulder pads protect the shoulders, they protect the collar bone, chest, ribs, back, and upper arms, too. They're made of hard plastic and dense foam with caps that shield the shoulders from direct hits.

⑬ Elbow Pads

People often use an elbow to break a fall and, since there are lots of falls in hockey, elbows pads are a must. The first elbow pads were made out of padded elastic bandages in 1910. Today, caps made of hard molded plastic protect the bony elbow tip, and the pads shield the forearm as well. Some also have air sacs to help absorb impacts.

Quick Shot

Women's hockey pants have narrower legs than men's, and women's gloves are designed to fit slimmer fingers and narrower palms. Grrls rule!

Quick Shot

Pro Alyn McCauley wears hockey's first one-piece helmet made of carbon and Aramid fibers (used in bullet-proof vests). Tests show that Alyn's helmet stands up under greater impacts over a longer period of time than plastic hockey helmets.

Goalie Gear

No other player needs as much protective gear as the goalie. He's bombarded with the puck all game long. In the early days, goaltenders wore no protective gear at all. They used the same sticks and skates as the other players. And they weren't allowed to hold the puck or kneel, lie, sit, or fall down on the ice. Talk about a tough job!

Today, goalies let in fewer goals than ever before. Why? Over the years, changes in the rules and improvements in goalie gear have changed the way goaltenders play the game. Now goalies wear a whopping 22 kg (50 lbs) of gear, and they cover more of the net just by standing still!

Quick Shot

Plastic, nylon, and foam have made goalie equipment lighter than leather. But these materials make it hard for the skin to breathe. So body heat builds up and goalies lose lots of water. That's why goalies are now allowed to keep a water bottle on top of the net.

1 Stick

Today, goalie sticks have a lie (see How to Tell a Lie, p. 29) that helps keep the blade flat on the ice, and a blade that's much wider than other players' sticks to help stop shots. Some goal sticks are made of carbon and graphite mixtures to reduce rebounds.

2 The Blocker

In the beginning, goalies wore gloves mainly for warmth. In the late 1940s, goaltender Frank Brimsek invented the blocker to deflect shots by taping a piece of plywood to the back of his glove. Eventually, a slablike blocker became part of goalies' standard gear. Today, the top part of the blocker is angled to direct rebounds away from the net and the surface is curved inward to cut down rebounds.

3 Skates

Goalie skates are designed to stop the puck. The small openings between the boot and blade don't let the puck through. The blades are almost flat with a shallow groove so goalies can move quickly from side to side.

4 Mask

After years of experimenting, many goalies now wear what's called a combination mask. It combines the freedom of a face-fitting mask with the protection of a helmet and built-in cage, without cluttering up the goalie's view of the action. Combination masks are custom-made for individual goaltenders out of light, strong materials, such as fiberglass, Kevlar, and graphite. The chin and forehead of the mask are shaped to deflect pucks away.

5 Chest Protector

This pad looks like a bulletproof vest. It combines a chest protector with shoulder pads made of strong, dense plastic. Air sacs line the chest area. They cushion shots by breaking up the energy at the point of impact and making it flow over a larger area.

6 Catching Glove

The catching glove stole on the scene in 1946 when goalie Emile Francis, who was also a baseball shortstop, began tending the net with a baseball mitt. Today, goalies' catching gloves are bigger than baseball mitts, and they're designed to quickly close around the puck.

7 Shin Pads

In the 1890s, some goaltenders wore leather goal pads used in the game of cricket, but the puck often bounced off the round corners of the cricket pads—straight into the net. In 1924, pads much like the ones used today were designed. But as goalies sweated and sprawled over the wet ice, the leather pads absorbed lots of water, becoming heavy and weighing goalies' legs down. In 1986 goalies began wearing pads made of light waterproof plastic, nylon, and foam. Today, some pads have foam inserts to help absorb shots and reduce rebounds.

No More Fishing for Goals

The net may have been the first piece of goal-judging equipment to enter the game. In the early 1900s, goal nets were made from fishing nets to catch the puck to try to stop the arguments that often erupted over whether a goal was scored. Back then, the rinks were dimly lit and defense players shot the puck up into the rafters to prevent the opposing team from scoring. And when the puck fell back to the ice, it was hard to tell whether it had landed between the two goal posts before it bounced away.

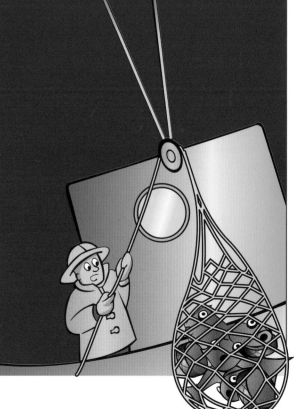

Jacques Plante

The Man Behind the Mask

Would you want to crouch between the pipes and try to stop shots without a facemask? Before Jacques Plante insisted on wearing a mask, goalies were expected to play bare faced.

Prompted by facial cuts, bruises, and fractures that he received in net, the star Montreal Canadiens goalie designed a fiberglass facemask. But his coach, Toe Blake, wouldn't let him wear it in games—maybe because the other face protector of the day, a clear plastic shield, fogged up and distracted goalies as the rink lights reflected in it

In 1959, New York Rangers forward Andy Bathgate took a shot on net, and it hit Plante in the face—wham!—slitting open a nasty cut. The game was stopped so Plante could have the cut stitched up. And he refused to return without his facemask. Blake didn't have another goaltender on the scene, and was forced to give in. Plante won the game in the facemask, and kept right on wearing it in a winning streak that led the Canadiens to win the Stanley Cup. Not long after that, all the goaltenders in the League began wearing facemasks. And the masks gave them protection to face shooters head on!

Chapter 6

The Complete Athlete

Whew! They'll huff and they'll puff and they'll chase the puck down! Hockey players are bigger, faster, and fitter than ever before. Is there something in the water? No—it's in the training, or conditioning. Thirty years ago, most professional players kept in shape just by playing hockey. They didn't train in the off-season. But in the Soviet–Canada series of 1972, North American coaches and players were forced to rethink. Russia nearly beat Canada! The Russians trained all year round, and their superior conditioning gave them an edge. They were able to play intensely without letting up, right through to the end of the games.

Hockey shifts may last only a minute, but they're one of the most vigorous workouts in pro sports! Players put out explosive bursts of speed to chase and carry the puck; they give and take bone-crunching body checks; they fight for the puck, pushing and shoving one another in the corners and along the boards; and sometimes they skate from end-to-end for an entire shift. So they need incredible endurance. That's why today's pros train all year round. How do players get their minds and bodies in tip-top playing condition?

Shape up! ➤

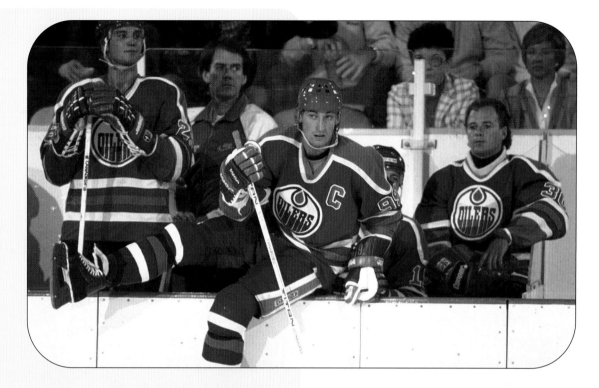

Flash 15 years into the future: you're a forward in the NHL. The game is tied 2–2 and the winning team wins the Stanley Cup. "Last minute of play," blares over the loudspeaker. With two other forwards out of the lineup with injuries, you've played more than your usual share of shifts. And this has been one fast-paced game. The coach gives you the nod and you hop over the boards. Do you have enough energy left to go all out for another shift? You bet! Thanks to the coaching staff's training program, you're in tip-top physical condition.

At the beginning of the season, the team's doctors gave you a complete medical exam. Your fitness, strength, flexibility, ability to relax, and heart efficiency were tested to find any weak spots. Then the coaching staff used the test results to design an individual training program to strengthen your weaknesses and get you into top shape.

If you weren't in such great shape, you'd be feeling pretty tired. Here's why. As you breathe, you take in the oxygen your body needs for energy. But when you play hockey, your body can't get that energy fast enough. So players need to train their bodies—by running, cycling, rollerblading, and lifting weights—to make the energy they need without oxygen.

The more physically fit you are, the longer you can play without getting sore muscles, and the faster your pace. Superior conditioning can help you outlast your opponents, even if they're stronger and more skilled. And so you can go all out in the last minute of play—and maybe score that game-winning goal!

Fuel Up

Food is fuel for the body. While the average person needs 1200 to 1500 calories from food a day, hockey players who train daily need 2000 to 5000. So the big leagues take food seriously! Junior players drafted by the Toronto Maple Leafs go to orientation camp for fitness tests—and cooking classes! Chefs teach the players how to make nutritious, easy-to-digest pre-game meals. Without a well-balanced diet, players may not have the energy they need and they may become susceptible to injuries.

Hockey players need to fuel up on carbohydrates, fats, and proteins, from each of the 4 food groups, in the following proportions:

- **60 to 65% carbohydrates:** Breads, cereals, pasta, fruit and vegetables give players their number one source of energy.

- **25% fats:** Cheese, yogurt, peanut butter, and salad oil give and store energy for players.

- **15% proteins:** Chicken, beef, fish, milk, and eggs help players' bodies grow and repair tissues.

Breads and cereals

Fruits and vegetables

Milk and cheese

Meat and fish

Tip

As the old saying goes, "how you practice is how you play." The more you practice, the more you develop your skills, so you can perform them effortlessly in a game. And the more you practice with your team, the more you learn how to play together. It's also important to play other sports that help develop your muscles, joints, flexibility, coordination, and physical fitness.

Quick Shot

Hockey can really take it out of you. During a game, pros can lose a whopping 2 to 4 kg (5–8 lbs)! This weight loss is mostly water. That's why it's important to drink fluids when you play.

Star ☆

When she was 15 years old, Hayley Wickenheiser was the youngest player to make Canada's national women's hockey team. She soon became one of the top women in the game. And in 1998 and 1999, she trained side-by-side with male NHL rookies.

Hayley Wickenheiser

Smack! Two players collide head on. Bam! A player's knee smashes into the boards. Whack! The puck hits a player in the arm. Hockey is a collision sport all right, and injuries are part of the game. But thanks to advances in sports medicine, players are recovering faster and better than ever before.

Fixing the Knee

Knee injuries are one of the top three hockey injuries. They are what forced Bobby Orr (photo, left) to hang up his skates for good, breaking the hearts of hockey fans everywhere.

Bobby Orr was a defense player like none before. Wayne Gretzky once said, "Every kid in the '60s and the early '70s grew up in Canada saying, 'I want to be like Bobby Orr.'" Orr played defense by going on offense! He won the NHL scoring championship not once but twice, radically changing the role of the defenseman in the game.

In his rookie year, Orr injured his knee and it was never the same. He tore the anterior cruciate ligament (ACL), which holds the thigh and shin bones together, and reinjured the knee several times.

Several operations later, his knee gave out, forcing him to retire in 1978 at the age of 29.

But medical science has come a long way since then. If Bobby Orr had injured his knee today, experts say it could be fixed. Doctors now have high-tech tools for the job. Unlike X-rays, which show bones, magnetic resonance imaging (MRI) uses radio waves to reveal tissues like ligaments and cartilage, so doctors can check them for damage. Doctors can use a tiny telescope, called an arthroscope, to look right inside the knee.

Once doctors see what the injury is, they can treat it. And if it requires surgery—to rebuild a torn ligament, for example—they use the arthroscope to look inside the knee as they operate. Arthroscopic surgery is less harmful to the knee than open surgery and takes less time to recover from. It's the bee's knees!

Doctors insert the arthroscope in the knee though a small cut and hook it up to a TV camera. The arthroscope shines light inside the knee and its lens magnifies the bones and tissues, which doctors see on a TV screen.

Quick Shot

One scientist who studied hockey collisions for 25 years thinks that some hits to the head, many of which are clean hits according to hockey rules, pack the power of a knockout punch.

Quick Fix in a Tube

When some pros need a quick injury fix, they climb into a rocket-shaped tube and seal it shut tight. And that's when the pressure to heal begins. No joke! Once inside, players sit under pressure that's twice as high as the normal air pressure you feel when you're outside. And they breathe 100% pure oxygen through a mask. The high pressure combines with the pure oxygen to pump lots of oxygen to the injury, which helps it heal faster. In fact, hyperbaric chambers like this can help players recover from bruised muscles, torn ligaments, and fractured bones in about half the usual time!

Conked in the Head

What do Eric Lindros and Paul Kariya have in common besides playing hockey?

They've both been knocked out of the lineup by a concussion—a chemical imbalance in the brain caused by a blow to the head. The human brain sits inside the skull like a person sitting in a car without a seatbelt. If your head gets hit, your skull stops or twists suddenly. Since the brain has nothing holding it in place, it crashes into the inside of the skull. Wham! This sets off a chain of chemical reactions that can cause dizziness, memory loss, headaches, balance problems—even personality changes or brain damage. But symptoms can be very subtle, which makes concussions hard to diagnose. Doctors just don't know what's going on in your head! So they don't know how to treat concussions. Until they unlock the mysteries of the human brain, the only cure is time.

The Mind

I magine this: your opponents are pounding shots on net. The puck bounces off the pads of your goalie and you pick up the rebound. Phew! But now what? Suddenly, you've got the puck. Whoa! A rush of excitement goes to your head. Boom! Before you know it, you've whacked the puck wildly down the ice and it lands on an opposing player's stick.

"Ugh, of all the bonehead moves…" you say to yourself. But don't get down on yourself. Several research studies show that athletes' thoughts and self-talk—things they say to themselves as they perform—influence their success. Researchers think that negative thoughts can lead to poor play, while positive thoughts can give players the chance to play well. So instead of focusing on what went wrong, focus on what went right—like the fact you cleared the puck out of your zone.

Mental training has recently become an important part of pro hockey. Just as players train their bodies, they train their minds. A sports psychologist helps players turn negative thinking habits into positive ones. Sports psychologists also help players learn skills, rehearse plays, and see success through the technique of visualization.

Visualization must be practiced like a physical skill. The idea is that, as you see mental pictures of moves and plays over and over, they take root in your mind. Then, when you're in a similar situation in a game, you instinctively make the imagined play successfully.

Studies show that visualization improves athletes' performances. In scientific experiments where one group of athletes gets physical training only and another group gets both physical and visualization training, the group with the visualization training outperforms the one who doesn't.

But visualization is not a sure-fire way to success. Scientists don't understand why it works for some players and not for others. Maybe someday in the future scientists will figure it all out. Until we understand more about it, all we can say is that the mind works in mysterious ways.

Soviet–Canada pre-game line-up, 1972

The Desire

Sure, you need good skating and puckhandling skills, good conditioning, and a good mental attitude to excel at hockey. But don't underestimate the power of desire. Think about this: the Russians had better skills, conditioning, speed, and teamwork in the 1972 Soviet–Canada series, so why did the Canadian team win? Some experts say that Team Canada's desire to win was stronger.

Though desire can't be measured like speed and strength, experts think it's a key ingredient of athletic success. In his book *Inside Hockey*, Stan Mikita says, "I have known a lot of players with exceptional talent who did not play as well as they should have. And I have seen men with less talent who have become outstanding players. The difference between them has been their degree of desire."

Goal-scoring superstar Paul Kariya uses visualization before every game. For example, Paul may imagine himself closing in on net, faking one way, then firing the puck past the goalie the other way. He thinks "the mind is the most important part of sports."

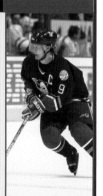

Paul Kariya

Quick Shot

Noisy crowds and stiff competition give some players a rush of the chemical adrenaline, which improves muscle power and action, providing the added spark to win.

Stumped by a Slump?

So you're a 50-goal-a-season guy or gal, but lately you can't seem to find the net. You've fallen into a slump. Sooner or later, it happens even to the best of the best. Most slumps are caused by staleness, or "burning out." Sometimes, players burn out from overtraining during a long, hard season, or from the build-up of stress they face both on and off the ice. Though staleness can show itself physically through loss of weight and appetite, many experts think it's more of a mental thing. To get out of a slump, some pros watch videos of their best goals or plays to rediscover all the little things they do that have made them successful before. It's important not to focus on things that are going wrong, but to focus on things that are going right— even if they seem like small things.

Legends of the Game

Wayne Gretzky

The Greatest One of All

Hockey has never seen a player the likes of Wayne Gretzky. The Great One put on his first skates when he was two years old, played hockey with ten-year-olds when he was six, and scored 378 goals in 68 games when he was ten.

Some people said he wasn't the greatest skater. They said he was too small and light for the NHL. They said his shot wasn't that hard. But when Gretzky turned pro, he broke almost every NHL scoring record in the book!

What made Gretzky truly great was his uncanny knack of anticipating what was going to happen next in the game. He always seemed to know where the puck was going to go or which teammate would be in the clear for a pass. This "sixth sense" was honed on a rink his Dad made in the backyard when Wayne was a kid. Wayne practiced for hours and hours and learned to "see" the ice, because he loved the game. And that's what made him the greatest one of all.

Chapter 7

The Science of Explosive Moves

Boom!

A hard slapshot misses the net by just centimeters and blasts into the boards. "Ohhh!" wail the fans. Ooof! A home team enforcer body checks a defense player who is trying to clear the puck and grinds him into the boards. Thud! "Whoo-hoo!" cheer the fans.

The slapshot and the body check are the two most exciting and explosive parts of hockey. The slapshot can turn the puck into the fastest-moving object in pro sports that will rip past a goalie faster than you can say, "She shoots. She scores!" And the body check is the most effective way to stop a player with the puck cold in his tracks. It can even send a player sailing into the boards or sprawling onto the ice with a force that's strong enough to break human bones.

What makes these parts of hockey so explosive? The energy that fuels them. Hang onto your seat and get set to take a look at the energy that gives a slapshot and a body check their "oomph."

Energize It!

The Slapshot

When a player fires off a slapshot, look out! It's the fastest shot in hockey. It can send the puck zooming at the net at 160 kilometers (100 miles) per hour—or more. Until the slapshot came along, most goals were scored with wrist shots that travelled no more than 100 km/h (60 mph). So goalies were able to track the puck with their eyes.

But right winger Bernie Geoffrion of the Montreal Canadiens' changed all that in the 1950s, when he and a few others invented the slapshot by winding up like a golfer and whacking the puck. When it slammed into the boards, the puck made a sound that earned Geoffrion the nickname "Boom Boom!" Soon, slapshots were booming all over the NHL, and goalies were suddenly bombarded by shots that moved too fast to see.

What makes a slapshot so fast? It's loaded with energy. Check out the split-second moves of a slapshot and see.

Setting Up the Puck

The more firepower, or energy, the player gives the puck, the faster it will go, and the harder it will be for the goalie to see! So she puts the puck in front of her, between her feet, where it can absorb the most energy.

Winding Up

With her weight on her back leg, the player raises her stick behind her as high as she can by lifting her back arm and turning her chest and hips. The farther she can draw back her stick, the more energy she can put into her shot—and the faster it will be.

Swinging Down

The player brings her stick down; shoulders, chest, and hips turn back the other way. As the stick hits the ice, 2–5 cm (1–2 in) behind the puck, her weight shifts to her front leg, transferring the force of her body weight into her stick—putting more energy into the puck.

Bending the Stick

The player puts pressure on the stick by pushing against its shaft and holding the upper end of it close to her body. This "loads" the stick with more energy. The shaft of the stick bends and stores this energy.

Slapping the Puck

The player sweeps her stickblade along the ice, pushing off on her back leg. This forces the power of her body weight into her stick and the puck, pushing it along a bit. The bent stick shaft snaps back, releasing its stored energy into the puck to give it more speed.

Following Through

The player keeps moving her stick forward and up. The puck can't absorb all the energy she loaded into the stick. So she must keep moving forward to absorb this energy and stay balanced. Or else she might fall over!

Secret Science of Passing

Passing the puck is another explosive part of hockey. It can move the puck down the ice two or three times faster than the speediest skater. How can you learn to pass accurately? Practice! Like Stephanie Boyd, a former Team USA center who plays in the Women's National Hockey League, hold your stick with "soft hands" or a loose grip, so it has some "give" to absorb the impact of the puck. Or else, Stephanie says, the puck might bounce off your stick. To avoid such a rebound, you also have to hold your stick at a right angle to the direction of the puck's travel. In fact, one study showed that most of the passes missed by receivers were fouled up because the receivers weren't holding their sticks at a right angle to the oncoming puck. Now that's a fact not to pass over!

Quick Answers to Speedy Questions

How do they know how fast a player's slapshot is?
Every year before the NHL all-star game is played, officials time players' slapshots with a radar gun.

Why is the speed of a shot so important?
The faster the puck goes, the less time the goalie has to prepare to stop it. And if the puck moves so fast that the goalie can't see it, chances are the goalie doesn't have a chance!

Why take slapshots without winding up all the way?
To get the shot away quickly. The more time players spend winding up, the more time the goalie has to get ready for the shot. So players "call the shots" case by case.

Quick Shot

The average NHL player weighs about 91 kg (200 lbs) and reaches speeds of 32 km (20 mi) per hour on the ice. The weight and speed give his body enough energy to light an average light bulb for almost 13 minutes!

Tip

Instead of going for the speed of a slapshot, try a wrist shot. One study shows that it is 40 percent more accurate than the slapshot. You can get a wrist shot away faster than a slapshot, because it takes less time to set up. And you can get a wrist shot off when you're in a traffic jam in front of the net.

The Physics of Body Checking

Here's the deal: the other team has swarmed into your zone. You're covering a forward who's on the point with the puck. Before he can get a shot away or pass to a teammate, you decide to take him out along the boards with a body check.

Throwing a body check requires lots of energy. And how much energy have you got to put into a body check? The total energy in your body is made up of your weight, or your potential energy, and the speed you're moving at, or your kinetic energy. Basically, the more you weigh and the faster you're moving, the more energy you've got. Check out how your energy goes to work in a body check to take out the opposition.

Getting the Power

The checker pushes hard off his back foot. This is where a body check's power comes from. The short burst of speed boosts his kinetic energy and helps him throw all his weight into the check. This means more energy to work on the "checkee."

The Hit

When the checker's shoulder hits the checkee, the checkee's body absorbs some or all of the checker's energy. The impact of the check usually shakes the checkee off the puck and sends him flying into the boards. Wham!

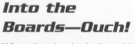

Into the Boards—Ouch!

When the checked player hits the boards, the energy from the check spreads out in the player's body. This bends the player "out of shape" along the boards. Some of the energy also goes into the boards.

The Snap Back

The boards give, or bend, a little as they absorb some of the energy from the checked player's body. Then they quickly snap back into place. This sends the energy back into the player and pushes him off the boards. Whoa, whammed again!

No Body Checks = Fast Game

Experts say that women's hockey is a faster game than men's. Why? Because there's no body checking allowed. Think about it: when you throw a body check, you slow down another player or stop him altogether. If he's got the puck, then sometimes the game slows down, too.

When players aren't hitting each other, a player's size and strength become less important. That means skills like stickhandling, nimbleness, and skating with speed to breaking away into open ice become even more critical. And that makes for a very fast and exciting game!

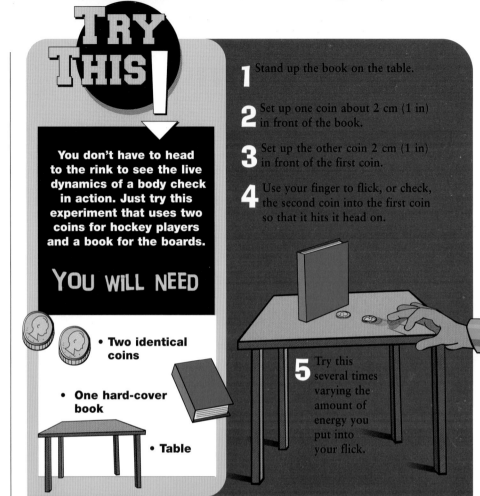

TRY THIS!

You don't have to head to the rink to see the live dynamics of a body check in action. Just try this experiment that uses two coins for hockey players and a book for the boards.

YOU WILL NEED

- **Two identical coins**
- **One hard-cover book**
- **Table**

1 Stand up the book on the table.

2 Set up one coin about 2 cm (1 in) in front of the book.

3 Set up the other coin 2 cm (1 in) in front of the first coin.

4 Use your finger to flick, or check, the second coin into the first coin so that it hits it head on.

5 Try this several times varying the amount of energy you put into your flick.

Did you notice that sometimes the checked coin strikes the checking coin when it bounces off the book? Sometimes that happens in hockey, too. A player gets hit. Oof! He slams into the boards. Bang! Then he bounces off the boards and bumps into the player who checked him. Ouch! Now that's a triple whammy!

Quick Shot

What makes giving a body check a dangerous move? Most pros say, "it's getting burned," because you're out of position. Not only does a body check take an opposing player out of the play, it takes you out of the play, too!

Bucko McDonald

The Ultimate Hit Man

His name was Bucko McDonald and he was a Detroit defenseman who played the game to hit. It was 1936 in the Montreal Forum. The Red Wings were playing the first game of a series against the Montreal Maroons, when Bucko dealt out a mind-boggling 37 body checks in just one game. Wham! Bam!

The hit man had "the perfect timing and conditions" on his side. The game went into an amazing six periods of sudden-death overtime. As the longest NHL game ever played dragged on, the ice turned slushy, and the skate-weary Maroons had an even tougher time staying out of Bucko's way.

Turns out Bucko had some unique motivation on his side. Before the game started, a Detroit fan offered him five dollars for every hit he made in the game. Little did the fan expect that Bucko would have an extra six periods of play to knock about. When it was all over, the hit-hungry fan owed the hit man $185!

Chapter 8

Shooter vs. Goalie

Click!

The official drops the puck on the ice to start the game. Now it's all about scoring goals.

Shooter: You've dreamed about this moment a thousand times. You're rushing down the ice on a breakaway. The only thing between the puck and the net is the goalie. Relax. You know what you're going to do; the goalie doesn't. So you have the edge.

Goalie: You've dreamed about this moment a thousand times. A shooter storms toward you on a breakaway. The only thing between the puck and the net is you. Stay cool. Stats say you stop many more pucks than not. So you have the odds on your side.

Shooter or goalie, it's a battle of skills— and wits. Are you ready?

Showdown
Dead Ahead ➤

The Shooter's Illusion

You're carrying the puck in on net. You've got it at your side, ready to shoot. Now, where to fire it? You look at the goalie and net and that's when you see the shooter's illusion—whether you know it or not. Sometimes, there's more net to shoot at than there appears. And sometimes, there's less!

The shooter's illusion is the difference between what you see and what the puck sees. When you carry the puck at your side, the puck has a different view of the net than you. Your eyes are a few feet above the ice, on your face, while the puck is down on the ice about a sticklength away from your body. And this difference creates an illusion.

In Front of the Net

What do you see? About the same amount of net on both sides of the goalie. But the puck, which is what you're aiming at the net, sees much more net on the goalie's stick side. So, shoot there. (Did you notice that the puck sees no open net on the glove side? Talk about you seeing an illusion!)

Good goalies like this one "play the angle," or face the puck—not the shooter—to block the shot. This changes the shooter's illusion and makes it work for the goalie. Now you see lots of net on the glove side. But the puck sees a much smaller opening there, and it sees net on the stick side which you don't see at all. So, in fact, you can shoot to either side.

On Your Wing

If the goalie lines up with you not the puck, you see more net on the short side (side of the net closest to you) than the far side. And the puck sees even more net on the short side, so shoot there.

If the goalie plays the angle right, you see lots of net on the far side. But the puck sees no net there. It sees net on the short side, which you may not see at all. (This is how playing the angle makes the shooter's illusion work for the goalie.) So shoot short side.

Tip

How do you aim the puck? Through your eyes. Keep your eyes on your target as you shoot. Don't worry that this may tell the goalie where you're shooting. Chances are the goalie will be watching the puck—not your eyes. And scientific research shows that watching your target can make your shot as much as 70% more accurate than watching the puck!

Quick Shot

To help stop goals from slipping past the goal judges, NHL officials check the nets before each game and each period of play to make sure there are no holes that the puck might fly through.

On Your Offwing

If the goalie lines up with you not the puck, you see net on the short side. But the puck sees more net on the far side. So shoot there.

If the goalie plays the angle right, you see net on the short side. But the puck sees net on both sides. So, you can shoot to either side.

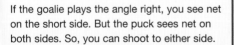

Net	⌒⌒	■ Goalie
Shooter	■	Shooter's vision
Puck	■	Puck's vision

TRY THIS!

You're zooming in on net with the puck. You spot the five-hole open between the goalie's legs. You shoot. You miss! There's only way to improve the accuracy of your shot. Practice, practice, practice! Try this target shooting drill and see.

YOU WILL NEED

Goal net • Hockey stick

Puck(s) • 5 empty tin cans

Nail • Hammer

String • Red paint

Paintbrush • Newspaper

Chalk (optional)

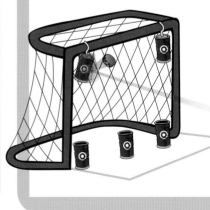

1 Place cans on newspaper. Paint them red and let dry.

2 Draw a bull's eye on each can.

3 Take two cans. Ask an adult to help you poke a hole through the bottom of each with the hammer and nail.

4 Thread a piece of string through each hole and knot it.

5 Hang these two cans in the top corners of the net by tying strings around the cross bar.

6 Place two cans in the bottom corners and center the last can between these two cans for the five-hole.

7 Choose a spot to shoot from and line up the puck(s). Pick one target, aim, and shoot the puck(s) at it.

8 Shoot at the other targets from the same spot in the same way.

9 Shoot at the targets from several other positions.

The Goalie's Angle

It's not easy being a human shield! Goalies have the toughest job in the game. You get pelted with flying pucks from every direction, and you're often blamed when a few slip past you—no matter how many you stop.

As modern-day hockey gets faster and the players more skilled, a goalie's job becomes even tougher. Today, nobody has to skate—forward, backward, and sideways—as fast as a goalie. And no player has to be as physically fit as a goalie. You need to play a full 60 minutes without regular breaks on the bench like your teammates get—and without losing your edge under 20 kg (50 lbs) of equipment.

Cutting Down the Angle

Luckily, you have an optical illusion you can use on that sharp shooter who's closing in on net. You can skate out of your crease to "cut down the angle," or reduce the amount of net a shooter can see. Here's how it works:

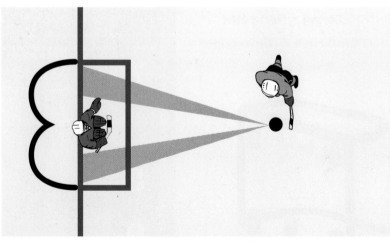

The deeper in net a goalie stays, the more net the shooter can see. Take a look—now, the shooter can see lots of net on both sides of the goalie.

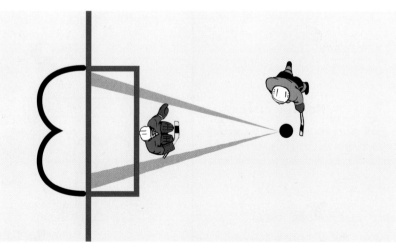

When the goalie moves out of the crease toward the puck, the shooter sees much less net. So the shooter has less net to shoot at. And that's the illusion.

Calling all goalies!
Try this experiment with a friend to see how to play the angle, or position yourself, to stop the shot. Playing the angles is one of the most important skills for goalies to develop.

YOU WILL NEED

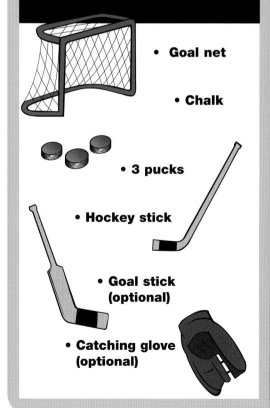

- **Goal net**

- **Chalk**

- **3 pucks**

- **Hockey stick**

- **Goal stick (optional)**

- **Catching glove (optional)**

1 On the ground outside, use the chalk to draw a goal line across the net.

2 Place one puck at the center of the goal line.

3 Hold the second puck in your hand, or catching glove. Stand or crouch in net.

4 Have your friend stickhandle the third puck to a spot in your defensive zone and then stop with the puck in full view.

5 Position your body directly in front of the shooter's puck. Imagine a rope connects the shooter's puck to the center of the net. Place one foot on each side of the imaginary rope.

6 Without looking behind you, come out of the net to cut down the angle, or give the shooter less net to shoot at.

7 Once you feel you're in the right position, place the third puck between your feet. Then step away.

8 Look at the three pucks. Are they in a straight line? If so, you've played the angle correctly and positioned yourself in the right spot for the shot. If not, you may have lined up your body with the shooter not the puck. Go back to step 5 and try this again.

9 Practice playing the angles. Have your friend stickhandle the puck to different spots and do these steps again.

Tip

Many shooters like to shoot to the goalie's stick side because goalies can move their gloves faster than their sticks. Take advantage of this—tempt shooters to your glove side by leaving more open net there. Sneaky!

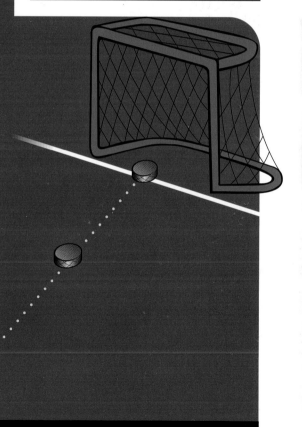

Hey, shooters. Do you see how the holes, or net areas, you're shooting at get smaller when the goalie comes out of the net to cut down the angle? Talk about taking your shot away!

The Breakaway Duel

Breakaways are exciting and nervewracking! Suddenly, it's just you against the goalie—or you against the shooter. All eyes are on you. The shooter's determined to put the puck in the net and the goalie is determined to keep it out. Playing a breakaway is like playing a bluffing game. So don't lose your nerve. Be prepared!

The Shooter

Know your opponent.

Does the goalie play stand-up or butterfly style? What are her weak points? Before every game, find out everything you can about the goalie. Then you'll be armed with the info you need for battle.

Look for clues and holes.

Watch the goalie. She can tell you how to beat her. Is she in or out of the net? Is she playing the angle right? (see The Goalie's Angle, p. 56)? Is her glove high or low? Is the five-hole open between her pads? What holes is she giving you to shoot at?

Make the goalie make the first move.

It's easier to beat the goalie if she makes the first move. She may even give you more net to shoot at! Force the goalie to move by faking a shot one way and then quickly shooting the other way. Or dribble the puck from side to side just before you shoot. Though this may not make the goalie move her body, she'll move her eyes as she watches the puck. And when the eyes refocus, they briefly blackout.

Shoot low.

A goalie can move her hands faster than her feet. Plus, low shots are the toughest shots for many goalies to handle, they're the easiest shots to aim, and they create better rebounds.

Follow your shot for rebounds.

Don't wait to see whether you score. Follow your shot so you can pick up a rebound and fire away again. Watch the goalie's pads for a rebound. Skate to where you think the rebound will go.

The Goalie

Know your opponent.

Does this shooter have a hotspot—a spot he shoots from time and time again? Does he like to deke, or fake a move to pull the goalie out of position? What are this shooter's favorite moves? Before every game, find out everything you can about opposing shooters. Then you'll have an idea of what to expect.

Track the puck.

Glue your eyes on the puck and don't let it out of your sight. Play the angle: turn your body to face the puck—not the shooter—straight on. Put as much of your body and equipment between the puck and the net as you can. Track the puck with your body. As the puck moves, move your body to keep facing the puck.

Make the shooter make the first move.

Remember: the shooter knows what he's going to do. You don't. Wait for him to commit to an action. The longer he takes, the more time there is for your teammates to get back to help you. Watch for clues that tell you when he's going to shoot. If he's carrying the puck in front of him, he has to draw it back to shoot. If he's carrying the puck at his side, he can shoot anytime. Sometimes, you can tempt the shooter by creating holes for him to shoot at. For example, you may open your pads for a moment then quickly close them when he shoots.

Cut down the angle.

Move out of your crease toward the puck to cut down the amount of open net there is to shoot at. As the shooter comes in, move back toward the net, so he can't deke you out of position. Cover the corner closest to the puck. But don't leave too much of the far side open—the shooter may make a break for it.

Don't give up rebounds.

Hold onto the puck or smother it. You can also angle your stick and your pads slightly toward the corners of the rink so the puck goes there—not in front of the net—when it bounces off them.

Star ☆

Are goalies crazy? 1950's goaltending great Glenn Hall played 502 regular season games straight, even though goaltending triggered his nervous stomach. Before most games and even between periods, he was often found throwing up his last meal!

Chris Osgood

Sharp Shooter Stopped Cold

April 1st, 1995: the Detroit Red Wings were leading the Dallas Stars 3–2 with less than a minute to go in the third period. The Stars stormed over the Wings' blue line, rushing in on goaltender Chris Osgood. In the rough-and-tumble play around the goal crease, the net sprang loose. The referee thought a Detroit player knocked it out of position to prevent the Stars from scoring. So he called the ultimate showdown between shooter and goalie—the penalty shot.

The Detroit Red Wings were not happy with the call, but Osgood didn't kick up a fuss. As Wings' Captain Steve Yzerman discussed the call with the ref, Osgood quietly scooped up some slushy snow around the goal posts and spread it over the ice in front of his crease. Maybe it was his idea of an April Fools' joke.

But the ref didn't notice and, as it turned out, Osgood was getting some extra puck-stopping action. When the Stars' Dave Gagner took the penalty shot, he went to deke Osgood, but the puck stayed glued to the spot. Instead of sliding on the slippery ice, the puck stuck in the slushy snow of Osgood's miniature snowbank. It looked as if Gagner completely flubbed the shot, and footage of the "blooper" played on TV over and over!

Rules and Regs

The Rink

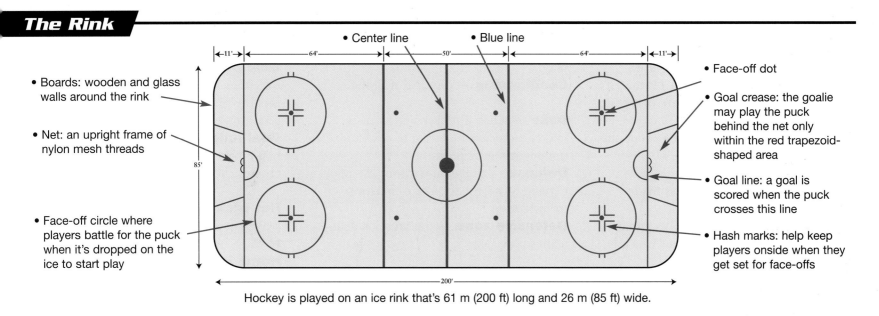

- Center line
- Blue line
- Face-off dot
- Goal crease: the goalie may play the puck behind the net only within the red trapezoid-shaped area
- Goal line: a goal is scored when the puck crosses this line
- Hash marks: help keep players onside when they get set for face-offs

- Boards: wooden and glass walls around the rink

- Net: an upright frame of nylon mesh threads

- Face-off circle where players battle for the puck when it's dropped on the ice to start play

Hockey is played on an ice rink that's 61 m (200 ft) long and 26 m (85 ft) wide.

The Players

- Defense player: his or her main job is to guard the team's defensive zone.
- Referee: the top official of the game.

- Winger: forward player who plays an outside position, left wing or right wing.
- Center: forward player who usually takes the face-offs for the puck.

- Goaltender: player whose main job is to keep the puck out of the net with his or her body and stick.

- Line official: an official on the ice who makes icing and offside calls, watches for illegal moves like tripping and holding, and drops the puck for face-offs.

How to Play

- The object of the game is to score goals by putting the puck in the net.
- The team who scores the most goals, wins.

- Each team may have no more than 6 players (usually a center, two wingers, two defense players, and a goalie) on the ice at all times.

- The game is played in three 20-minute periods with 15 minutes of intermission between each.

- If the score is tied at the end of the third period, the game goes into "sudden-death" overtime. If no goal is scored after 5 minutes, a shootout decides the game.

ACL — anterior cruciate ligament, which is commonly injured in hockey; it's connecting tissue, which holds the shin and thigh bones together, in the knee

Assist — a point given to a player for passing the puck to a teammate to set up a goal that has been scored

Attacking zone — the area inside the opponent's blue line

Backhand — a shot or pass made with the back of the stickblade

Banana blade — a massively curved stickblade that's illegal now but was all the rage in the '60s

Between the pipes — a goalie's position between the goalposts in net

Breakaway — when a player carrying the puck gets a scoring opportunity with no defending players between him/her and the opposing goalie

Blade — the sharp, steel runner on the bottom of a skate; the bottom part of a hockey stick that contacts the puck

Body check — using the hip or shoulder to slow down or block an opponent who has the puck

Butterfly style goalie — tends net with knees together and feet slightly apart, so he/she can quickly fall to his/her knees to make saves and then easily get back up on his/her feet

Changing on the fly — substitution of players while the game is being played

Check — to take a player off the puck or away from the play

Coach — the person who manages the team during practices and games, sets team strategy, and chooses which players play

Conditioning — physical training

Deke — when a player with a puck makes a quick fake to try to trick an opponent out of position

Defense — the team without the puck; playing to try to stop the opposition from scoring

Defensive zone — the area inside a team's blue line

Enforcer — a tough player who fights

Face-off — when two opposing players face each other and battle for the puck once it's dropped on the ice to start play

Far side — the side of the net that's the farthest away from a shooter

Fake — moving your body in one direction to try to make an opponent think you're going that way and then going another way

Five hole — the area between a goaltender's legs

Forehand — a shot or pass made with the front of the stickblade

Forward — a center, right wing, or left wing player whose main job is to try to score goals

Glove side — the side of the net where the goalie has a catching glove to stop shots

Goal — when the puck crosses the goal line. Teams get one point for each goal scored.

Goal posts — one of two upright posts on either side of the net. When the puck hits the goal post, it is not counted as a goal or a shot on goal.

Goal judge — an official who sits right behind the net to see when the puck crosses the goal line

Hat trick — three goals scored by one player in a single game

Hits — body checks

Home ice — a team's hometown rink

Hybrid goalie — a goaltender who tends net using a combination of butterfly and standup goalie styles

Ice — the slippery surface on which the game is played

Icing — when a team shoots or deflects the puck from behind the center line past the other team's goal line. Play is stopped and a face-off held in the defensive zone of the team who shot the puck. The team that iced the puck cannot make a line change before the face-off.

Lie — the angle between a stick's blade and shaft

Line — three forwards—usually a center and two wingers—who regularly play together

Linemate — one of two players with whom a forward regularly plays

Lineup — a list of a team's players who are dressed to play a game

Netcam — a tiny TV camera inside the net that gives TV audience a close-up view of net action and helps goal judges decide whether a goal has been scored

NHL — National Hockey League of professional teams in Canada and the US

Offense — the team who has the puck; methods or plays to try to score goals

Offside — when a player enters the attacking zone before the puck. Unless the player returns to the blue line and "tags" it, play is stopped and a face-off is held outside the attacking zone.

On the road — when a team is playing away from their hometown rink

Overtime — play after the third period of a tied game

Pass — shooting the puck to a teammate

Penalty — when a player is punished for breaking a rule by having to leave the ice

Penalty box — where players sit off the ice when they get a penalty

Period — one of three 20-minute intervals of play in regulation game time

Playoffs — an end-of-season NHL tournament in which teams compete to win a silver cup trophy called the Stanley Cup

Point — the area just inside the offensive blue line near the boards

Power play — when a team has more players on the ice than its opponent because a penalty (or penalties) have been called against its opponent

Puck — a black, round rubber disk players try to put in the net

Pull the goalie — when a team takes their goalie off the ice to put an extra player on instead to try to score a goal, usually in the last couple of minutes of a game

Rebound — when the puck bounces off the goalie back into play after a save

Scoring race — a competition between players to rack up the most points in a season, in which one point is awarded for each goal and each assist a player makes

Shift — a player's turn out on the ice during the game; most pro shifts last from 40 seconds to a minute

Shorthanded — when a team is forced to play with less than six players on the ice because one or more have been sent to the penalty box

Short side — the side of the net that's closest to a shooter

Shot on goal — a shot stopped from going in the net by the goalie; note that shots that go wide of the net or hit the net's goalposts are not counted as shots on goal

Shutout — when a goalie plays a whole game without letting in any goals

Slapshot — shooting the puck with a big backswing and a sweeping motion

Slot — the area directly in front of the net, from the goal crease to the top of the face-off circles

Standup goalie — a goaltender who stays on his/her feet and keeps his/her pads together; a goaltending style opposite to the butterfly style

Stanley Cup — a trophy—a silver cup named after Lord Stanley who donated it—given to the winning team of the NHL playoffs

Stick — a piece of wood, metal, or high-tech material, with a blade at the bottom, which players use to shoot the puck

Stickhandle — controlling the puck by rapidly shifting the puck from one side of the stickblade to the other

Stick side — side of the net where the goalie has a wide stick to stop shots

Visualization — mentally planning or rehearsing moves like shooting or passing in order to do them that way instinctively when you play

Wing — the left side or right side of the rink, left wing or right wing

Wrist shot — shooting with the puck directly against the blade of the stick

Zamboni — a machine that resurfaces the ice between games and periods

Index

Photo Credits

Answer to "Try This" page 25: The puck at room temperature bounces higher than the one that was chilled in the freezer. So chances are you'd rather play with the chilled puck because it bounces less, which makes it easier to control.